BabyGym

BabyGym

BRAIN AND BODY GYM FOR BABIES

Dr Melodie de Jager

METZ PRESS

This edition published by Metz Press in 2009
1 Cameronians Avenue
Welgemoed, 7530 South Africa

First published in 2004 by Human & Rousseau

Publisher	Wilsia Metz
Design & lay-out	Liezl Maree, Blue Berry Advertising
Illustrations	Izak Vollgraaff
Proofreader	Deborah Morbin

Printed and bound by Paarl Print, Dal Josafat, Paarl
ISBN 978-1-920268-16-9

To:
Prachant J. Anthofer for creating a space where people
can rest and where thoughts and dreams can be born;
Joe Bettoni for apples, candles and scorpion removals;
Nina Wasserman for juggling with a smile;
Ruan, Waldo & Cozette for having me as their mom.
Deo Gloria

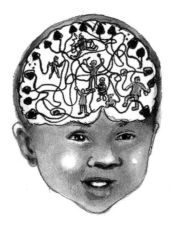

Contents

BabyGym – Brain and body gym for babies

Boy or girl?
To avoid the cumbersome practice of using *he* or *she* and *his* or *her* in every instance to show that the baby could be either a boy or a girl, *he* and *she* are used alternately in different sections of *BabyGym*.

Contents

BabyGym Institute

For more information and classes in your area, contact the BabyGym Institute:

53 8th Street
Linden
Johannesburg
South Africa

Tel: +27 82 301 5860
Email: institute@babygym.co.za
Website: www.babygym.co.za

BabyGym – Brain and body gym for babies

Introduction

Within minutes after a baby animal is born, it struggles to its feet, and makes a beeline for Mom, instinctively knowing that she is the source and carrier of its first meal. Now, that is pretty advanced brain functioning when compared to the way a newborn baby reacts …

A newborn baby's brain is well developed to survive in the safe, warm, moist and nourishing environment of the womb, but the brain is not developed enough to function in any meaningful way in the real world. The similarity between a newborn animal and a baby lies in their 'struggle' to get up and to get going. It's in struggling to get up that they develop all the skills and abilities necessary to survive outside the womb.

I am reminded of the experience of a novice ostrich farmer who eagerly awaited his first hatch of ostriches. He heard them pecking away from inside the shells for days on end and, feeling sorry for them, he decided to come to their rescue – by merely lending a hand to make it easier for them. With a teaspoon he gently tapped in sync with the ostriches' pecking to soften the eggshells and hasten the hatchlings' entrance into the world. When they started breaking through the shells he was astonished to see that they were all born with floppy necks! He waited patiently for days for their neck muscles to strengthen, but in vain. He consulted an experienced ostrich breeder who told him that his 'help' in minimising their struggle to get out was what had caused their weak neck muscles. They needed the struggle to become independent, proud, strong-necked ostriches!

BabyGym guides parents and other primary caregivers in ways to optimise baby's struggle to learn through exploiting the vital early-life opportunities. It shows you how to make every parent/child moment count.

I see *BabyGym* as an operator's manual, specifically geared towards baby's brain development, for parents-to-be or new parents. The book was born from

BabyGym – Brain and body gym for babies

my many years of experience as the mother of Ruan, Waldo and Cozette, my work as a learning facilitator and intensive research into learning excellence.

Enjoy the marvellous gift of a newborn baby and the mind-expanding growth opportunities it offers Mom and Dad! And should you have to stand in for an absent parent for shorter or longer periods, the joy can be as intense.

Warm regards

institute@babygym.co.za
www.babygym.co.za

Where is the instruction manual?

When asked what they would wish for most, new parents invariably answer: Sleep, and an instruction manual.

When the eagerly-awaited bundle of joy is finally placed in your arms, you are often overwhelmed with the most intense feelings of helpless frustration, precisely because babies don't come with instruction manuals. And should you be charged with caring for someone else's infant these feelings are compounded by the responsibility you feel towards the natural parents. When you get a new kettle, TV, patio set or even instant noodles, they're accompanied by complete instructions. But what about the instructions on: **How to raise your beautiful new baby**? What are the do's and don'ts? Where do you start and what must you watch out for?

Becoming, and being, a mom or dad, represents one of the most valuable and meaningful investments in time, energy and money you will ever make! But how do you go about it?

The moment you become a parent, you become an artist. Artists have vision, they have passion, they sculpt and they form. Artists tweak a little here and add a little there. They don't always know exactly **how to**, but their instinct leads them to rework the raw materials into a final product nobody has ever seen.

Being a mom or a dad, or a substitute caregiver, may be compared to being an artist. Have vision, be passionate, trust your instincts and you will sculpt and form the character and future of a walking 'piece of art'.

BabyGym is a guide to **thinking about the basics** to ensure that your millennium baby grows up as a happy, confident whole-brain kid.

BabyGym – Brain and body gym for babies

A BABY'S PERSPECTIVE

During natural development *in utero*, baby's every need is being met – baby is safe, warm, being fed and needs no cleaning. It is surrounded by Mom's rhythmic heartbeat and the soothing sounds of her breathing and digestion (if she doesn't have indigestion or heartburn!). A baby feels at one with the world and confident about its role in it. In the absence of competition a baby cannot be compared, evaluated, labelled or judged as being different. A baby *in utero* just **is**.

A stabilising anchor

But the moment a baby is born, this peaceful existence is shattered. What a shock – lights are blinding, air is cold, sounds are loud and jarring, material on

Where is the instruction manual?

the skin feels strange and Mom is no longer constantly and comfortingly right there. Just imagine yourself in such a situation …

Wouldn't you feel abandoned and all alone, as though everything you hold dear has been ripped away? You would feel afraid and very vulnerable. You would probably yell your head off if someone should smack you on the buttocks to ensure you clear your passageways of any amniotic fluid! Can you imagine how bewildering it must be? Remember, you have never seen another human being, you have never looked at yourself in a mirror (for all you know you are one big round ball!).

Talk about stress levels – a newborn baby's stress levels would probably be comparable to those of an adult experiencing several major life-changing events simultaneously!

Luckily, a human baby's brain always comes to the rescue. Very soon the brain receives impulses to adapt to the new surroundings by developing the ability to recognise Mom's smell while focusing the eyes and adjusting the hearing to register Mom and Dad's faces and voices.

The moment you can pick Mom and Dad out from others, you have a stabilising anchor amongst all the impressions and changes. You feel safe once again.

Or at least until you experience your first pangs of hunger – remember, *in utero* you had a constant **on-line food supply**. Can you imagine feeling a strange, uncomfortable sensation more or less in the middle of your body and not knowing what it means? Because you can only know what you have experienced, and talk about what you have labelled, how frightening hunger pangs must be – not to mention the sensation of wetting your nappy or burping. It is no wonder that in therapy people often deal with a rebirthing process to minimise the trauma stemming from birth!

It is not only the baby who experiences shock – being a first-time parent is an ambivalent experience: you feel excited, proud and grateful, but also helpless, vulnerable and frustrated because you can't communicate with your baby and do not understand your baby's language. Substitute caregivers may also be concerned that they lack the instinctive feel for what baby wants.

BabyGym – Brain and body gym for babies

BABY LANGUAGE IS BODY LANGUAGE

Babies talk, but not in words. Babies 'talk' through movement, actions and a variety of cries. They want to help you care for them by expressing their needs, because development and learning are about the fulfilment of needs. All **learning** is about the need to survive. The need to survive as a human being is driven by:

- the need to be somebody, and
- the need to be accepted by others.

To satisfy these two driving needs, the brain comes to the rescue.

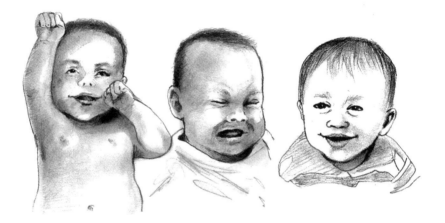

Baby language is body language

The brain comes to the rescue because needs evoke intense spurts of enthusiasm that trigger the brain to respond by creating neurochemical pathways to fulfil the need to be fed, cleaned, burped and held. Because these needs were automatically met *in utero*, the brain now has to **develop** new skills and abilities to have these requirements met.

Where is the instruction manual?

The sensory-motor process:
The far senses are stimulated by
sounds, sights, smells and taste, while
bodily position, muscle tension and
movement are perceived through the
near senses. The little girl employs her
muscles to sit upright, hold the flower
and bring the ice cream to her mouth.

How does the brain know what to respond to and what to develop? It knows as a result of a complex **sensory-motor** process. **Sensory** process refers to the baby's far and near senses. Far senses are those that respond to what is happening in the environment – touch, smell, taste, sight, hearing – while near senses are those that respond to what is happening inside the body, and include the vestibular (balance), proprioceptive (for the detection of the motion or position of the body or a limb) and kinesthetic systems. **Motor** process refers to action – through movement, sound or speech.

In utero the baby felt at one with Mom, and Mom was its whole world. The moment the baby is born, he or she is separated from Mom/the world and desperately needs a way of reconnecting to feel safe and secure. This is where the

BabyGym – Brain and body gym for babies

baby's innate sensory-motor capacity comes to the rescue. Once it is stimulated and developed, the sensory-motor system acts as a communication network, linking the baby and the environment.

The workings of the sensory-motor system is illustrated by the example of you encouraging your little one to wave to Granny and Grandpa when they take their leave after a visit. You know your child can wave, but there is no response … No matter how many times you prompt, still no response. It's only once they have disappeared round the corner that the little hand starts waving! What happened, why are baby's responses so slow?

> ### Did you know
> the brain is an infinite reservoir of potential that lies dormant until a need is developed?

IT'S ALL IN THE NEUROCHEMICAL WIRING

When all goes well during the pregnancy, the brain of a newborn baby retains the structural and developmental genes that it was endowed with at conception to programme the building and development of the brain.

Brain building occurs through the division of neurons (the cells that carry the messages between parts of the brain through biochemical reactions to receive, process and transmit information). When a baby is born the brain has dramatically more neurons than it will ever have later in life. Thereafter, the unused neurons start dying: lack of exercise results in them atrophying and fading away.

Even though the number of neurons start decreasing after the first year, the brain is continuously expanding. Brain growth is the result of the genetic programme within these neurons, which means that every baby is born with a **programme to succeed and prosper in life**!

This genetic programme instructs the neurons to increase in size and to send out many branches to make connections, called synaptic connections, with other neurons. Some of this branching and connecting is genetically programmed to happen *in utero* (survival patterns like heartbeat, breathing, and some of the reflexes), but most of the connecting happens at a tremendous pace once a baby is born. These branches (dendrites and axons) and their protective cellular wrapping (myelin) are what causes the several-fold increase in brain size and mass between birth and adulthood. Because of the many different branches reaching out from each neuron, messages can be received (sensory input) and sent (motor output) to many other neurons simultaneously. The more the synaptic connections are exercised, the stronger and more stable they will become. Current research indicates that these neurochemical networks enable feeling, thought and skills.

Now this is where the **struggle** and **needs** referred to earlier come in. When babies sense needs such as a hunger pang, a dirty nappy or a desire to wave to Grandpa and Grandma, they want their needs satisfied immediately. This impatience creates a sense of excitement, which signals to the brain that a response is needed, and the branching of neurons is activated. But branching is no simple task. It is like walking through dense bushes – a way needs to be forged and forging takes time! When baby hears you say, "Wave to Grandpa and Grandma", an impulse is received by the ear and sent to the brain. It can

BabyGym – Brain and body gym for babies

only get to the brain if there is a network connecting the outer ear to the hearing centres in the brain. Now the brain processes the instruction to wave (if there is a supporting network to think) and sends an instruction to the hand to respond. If the babies have not yet discovered their hands, they cannot wave. As strange as it may sound, babies are not born with the knowledge that they have hands and that they can control their hands! Babies need to discover their hands, build networks between the brain and hands and then learn to control the hands via these neurochemical networks before they can wave. No wonder human babies have the longest childhood of all living beings – they need their childhood to develop the supporting structures and networks to enable them to read, write and solve problems later in life.

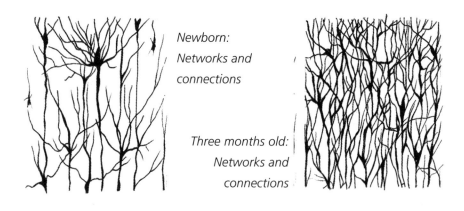

Newborn:
Networks and
connections

Three months old:
Networks and
connections

It is stimulation and development of this sensory-motor loop that later result in babies experiencing their surroundings, reaching milestones and developing the whole brain.

Your baby, like all babies, starts life as an active and eager learner with an innate desire to explore and discover, and you can help this process along with love and stimulation.

Where is the instruction manual?

Experience means being fully aware of something through employing all of the senses. Therefore, stimulating the senses is the first step in waking up the sensory-motor system. Every moment of the day your baby's skin, ears, eyes, nose and mouth are stimulated by the environment which aids the development of his/her far senses. These senses are called **far senses** because they collect impressions and sensations from 'outside' of baby (which to baby feels like **far away**) and bring them into baby's awareness to create experiences.

> **Babies can only learn what they have experienced**
> No experience = no learning
> Limited experience = limited learning
> Plenty of experience = plenty of learning

Babies don't only want to know what is happening outside of their bodies, but also what is happening 'inside' the body. The brain needs sensory input from inside the body to be able to act on a baby's needs. To feel safe and secure your baby needs to be able to sense himself and where he is in space. Sensing the

BabyGym — Brain and body gym for babies

self means being aware of pleasure, contentment, fullness, hunger, pain, tiredness, discomfort, whether it is upside down, falling, in danger and much more. Sensory input from inside the body is produced by the **near senses**. The near senses include the sense of movement (kinesthetics), balance (vestibular system) and proprioception (where the body is in space).

One tends to take so many skills for granted that it is mind-boggling to think that a baby doesn't know where he is in space (spatial orientation). Being born is like moving from a rural farm to a big city. You don't know where you are or what is where. To orientate yourself, you need a fixed point of reference (address or landmark), a map and some directions and then the opportunity to just get out there and do it.

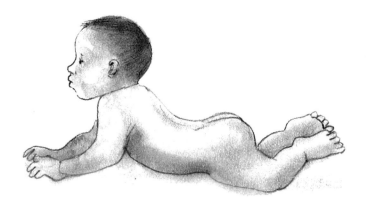

Your newborn baby needs exactly the same help as a relocated adult: he needs a fixed point of reference, a map/some directions and then the opportunity to get out there and do it. *BabyGym* is a simple and practical guide on:

1. How to establish a fixed point of reference,
2. How to draw a map and give directions,
3. How to create opportunities for baby to get out there and do it.

Where is the instruction manual?

These three steps will be applied in *BabyGym* to optimally stimulate your baby's body and sense of self, language development, emotions and thinking – making every available moment count. The same principles underlying the brain and body exercises for improving and maintaining the fitness of the adult brain (see the books *Mind Moves®* and *Mind Dynamics®*) are applied for developing and exercising the infant brain.

STIMULATION IS BRAIN FOOD

A baby would rather learn than eat, because learning comes naturally to a child. However, children do need abundant stimulation, exposure and experience to excite the senses and the brain to enable them to learn with ease.

Scientists have discovered that a baby's environment not only serves as a favourable context for development, but that a stimulating environment may be seen as the food that determines how the brain will grow through forming its networks. New technology can determine and map how the sounds babies make, the songs they hear, and the games they play have a direct impact on which connections and networks will form the intricate brain circuitry that kids carry with them into school, and later into adulthood.

The baby's 'struggle', like that of the baby ostrich, is not so much a struggle as a drawn-out game played over and over, resulting in the mastering of skills and need fulfilment.

BabyGym – Brain and body gym for babies

When a child is stimulated by seeing Mom's bobbing face, a connection is formed between the eyes and brain. Each time baby sees Mom's face, that connection is strengthened and, if reinforced often enough, it becomes a permanent memory and gets protected for future use by myelin (the fatty sheath surrounding the cellular connections).

Did you know
a baby's recognition of Mom's face is hard-wired by the third month?

Where is the instruction manual?

How many times did the baby see Mom's face before it became permanently imprinted in the brain? Probably thousands of times. It is in the repetition of actions and the mastery of these actions that the newborn baby's need to become someone, and to be accepted by others is being met. The better your baby becomes at a task, the more positive the feedback you give him, the more he will glow and grow.

It is the brain's plasticity that enables babies and kids to adapt, change and recover from trauma, but you need to catch the windows of opportunity when optimal learning can take place. If a baby doesn't receive certain kinds of stimulation within these critical timeframes, forging connections and networks later becomes more difficult. It is never impossible to forge connections, but it becomes markedly more difficult.

WHAT IS A WINDOW OF OPPORTUNITY ?

A window of opportunity is the prime time (milestones) that marks a little one's developmental progress. For example, motor skills progress rapidly in kids during the first eighteen months and the window for learning language is in the first six years.

In the development of a baby four major windows of opportunity exist:

- Opportunity to develop the **body** (neurochemical networks, muscle strength, muscle co-ordination, balance and the senses);
- Opportunity to develop **feelings and emotions**;
- Opportunity to develop **language**;
- Opportunity to develop **thinking**.

BabyGym – Brain and body gym for babies

Physical development

I HAVE A BODY

The first window of opportunity is for baby to discover her own body as a **fixed point of reference**. In the constant changes and movement around the baby, the stabile and constant reference point (that which is **always** present) is her own body. Do not forget that your baby doesn't know what she looks like and doesn't know what she can do. Therefore Step 1 for new parents is to make your baby aware of her own body. Where babies are in substitute day care, the carer would do well to implement these principles whenever the opportunity presents itself.

> ### Did you know
> that most babies are born with well-developed hearing and that a baby's ability to learn a language is determined pre-birth? While still in the womb your baby hears the frequencies and vibrations of language that develop the ears' range of hearing, which enables her to recognise her mother tongue after birth.

Bear in mind that, because of constricted space and the absence of light, the baby could only rely on its near senses and sense of hearing while still *in utero*.

The baby moved about and heard a lot pre-birth, so recognising Mom's language and voice is soothing and creates a sense of safety, which gives it a sense of stability and security. But being born is to learn and grow by discovering the other senses and learning how to use them to become self-aware and promote self-acceptance.

Did you know
many adults reject themselves because they never 'bonded' with their own bodies soon after birth?

Bonding with the body requires:

- A relaxed body,
- Wide-awake senses, and
- Strong muscles.

HOW TO RELAX YOUR BABY

A newborn baby is generally in a scrunched-up and protective posture. The back, fingers and toes are curled up and the knees are drawn in under the tummy, while the neck is turned sideways. This is the baby's space-saving posture and the residual of months in the womb. The baby also automatically assumes this posture as this is the position the muscles know, and therefore the baby's muscle memory is that of the prone foetal position. She mimics the *in utero* posture to feel safe and secure.

Physical development

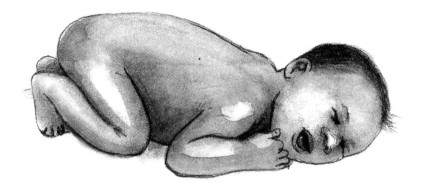

To do

- Gently sway, rock, stroke and sing or talk to your baby to simulate her *in utero* experience, thus making the transition from being one with Mom to being separated from Mom easier.

Did you know
the skin is the largest organ in the body?

- It is therefore crucial that you massage your baby's whole body as the skin is baby's highway to relaxation and getting to know her own body. Every time you touch your baby the receptors in the skin send a message to the brain to say, "This arm, tummy, back, leg or foot is a part of you." This is the beginning of your baby's self-image.

- There are excellent courses and books available specialising in baby massage (listed at the back of the book). The underlying principle is that you gently, and slowly, want to unfold and straighten the muscles by stroking the arm from the shoulder to the tips of the fingers, and the leg from the hip to the tips of the toes.
- When you are changing a nappy or bathing your (or someone else's) little one you can slowly and gently start opening up the hands by stroking from the wrist to the tips of the fingers, one finger at a time.

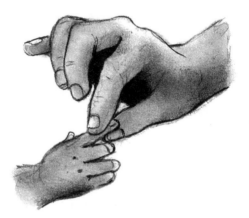

- You can uncurl the feet and toes by gently and slowly stroking the feet from the heel to the toes, while pulling your fingers along the sole, ending by unfolding each toe on its own.
- Massage the head and face all over in small, circular movements.
- Because your baby is used to your voice and responds well to singing and talking, use your voice to communicate with your little one, naming the body parts you are massaging, expressing how much you love them and how well they are going to do in life.

Physical development

HOW TO WAKE UP THE SENSES

Waking up the senses is every bit as technical as adjusting the antenna on your TV – it is about tuning in to receive the signals for producing a crystal clear image.

Stimulation of the skin, nose, taste buds, ears, eyes, as well as stimulation of the near senses through movement, creates signals that tickle the senses to wake up. Once the senses are alert, the tickling is transformed into electrical impulses that run via neurochemical pathways to the brain. These impulses are then reconstructed in the brain to create a representation of the original experience. It's like an image on a TV screen – the image is not the original real-life situation, but a representation thereof. What you watch on the screen depends on the quality of the signal (acuity of the senses) and the accuracy of the representation (reconstructed in the brain).

If the eyes are not working properly yet, the visual image would be out of focus, the colour may be dull and the contrast blurred. If the ears are not working optimally, the sound would be too soft or too loud, too deep or too high to fall within baby's range of hearing. If the taste buds are still developing, the baby would be indifferent to a variety of tastes or overly sensitive to certain tastes. If the nose is not yet doing its job fully the baby may be oblivious to smells. If the sensory receptors in the skin are not well developed, the baby may not register pain or pleasure, or the brain may register even the most subtle tactile sensation as extreme irritation, causing baby to display tactile defensiveness and avoidance of contact at all costs.

WAKING UP THE MOUTH

The mouth is the predominant sense organ in a newborn baby and accounts for babies' preference to stick everything in their mouths. The mouth represents a large area in the brain and when the mouth is stimulated, so is the corresponding area in the brain.

BabyGym – Brain and body gym for babies

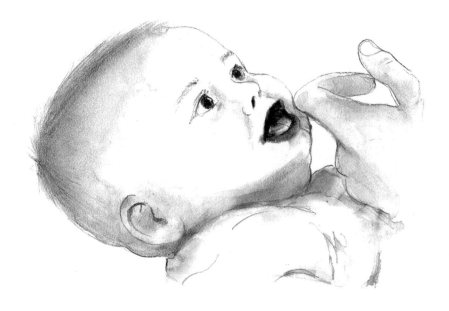

In combination, the baby's mouth, lips and tongue also act as a source of nourishment and pleasure. As a result of the rooting reflex (the reflexive search for a nipple), the baby would naturally turn her mouth towards the stimulation, searching for the food source when her cheek is stroked. The moment the mouth finds the cause of stimulation, which can be a finger, nipple or teat, the sucking reflex takes over to explore further. Every sucking action is not a quest for food; babies also suck for pleasure. While the baby suckles, her tongue pushes against the hard palate, which stimulates the limbic system or (emotional) part of the brain. Sucking thus promotes the secretion of feel-good hormones, which in turn promotes relaxation and boosts the immune system.

In addition to this, sucking develops the facial and tongue muscles needed for clear speech and correct formation of sounds. Sucking also helps to drain excess fluid from cranial cavities, thus reducing the chances of ear infections and sinusitis.

Physical development

It is important to note that, allowing for individual differences, the baby's sucking reflex will inhibit at around four months. This means that she has repeated the action enough times and sucking, and what to suck, become conscious choices rather than reflexive behaviour. This also means that you no longer need to stimulate this reflex.

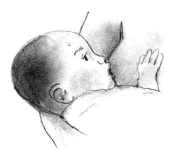

To do

- To promote the sucking reflex, touch baby's chin with one hand and baby's belly button with your other hand. Gently massage both points simultaneously. Remember that the umbilical cord was the original source of nourishment and stimulating both points simultaneously encourages the transition from being fed to feeding.

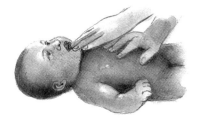

- You can also gently, and simultaneously, massage between top lip and nose with the one hand and baby's coccyx (tail-bone) with the other to stimulate the sucking reflex and promote metabolism.

- Gently draw the outline of the lips with your finger, a cotton bud or feather.
- Massage jaw joints just below the cheeks in a circular motion for relaxation.

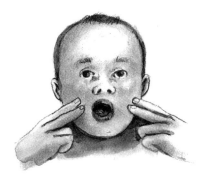

BabyGym – Brain and body gym for babies

WAKING UP THE NOSE

Like most animals, babies employ their sense of smell to protect themselves. They recognise Mom first, initially by her smell and her voice, and Dad later, also by his smell and his voice. That's why it is often recommended that you use the same perfume for a while till your little one has the ability to recognise you in another way.

To do

- For the first few weeks, keep smells the same in as far as possible to create a feeling of familiarity.
- When taking baby for a stroll in the garden, touch the nose and then bring baby closer to a flower. Keep an eye out for any allergic or avoidance reactions.
- When cooking and cleaning, give a whiff of the smells but be careful of bringing strong scents too close to the nose. The membrane in the nose is still thin and strong smells can burn it.
- There are exquisite scratch and smell books, but books, television and computers are second best – always opt for the real thing first. Babies can only learn what they experience, so the more senses are involved in an experience, the greater the quality of the learning.

Physical development

WAKING UP THE EARS

Hearing, a sense of balance, memory and critical thinking skills are all proc-
essed in the temporal-lobe area around the ears. As mentioned earlier, hearing
develops pre-birth to enable your baby to orientate herself more quickly after
birth. Hearing is a baby's lifeline with Mom and Dad, and therefore there is no
substitute for a loving human voice.

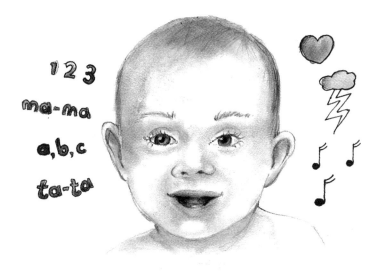

Every baby is born with a dominant ear – an ear she prefers to use. The left ear
is the more musical, emotional and tonal ear, while the right ear is the more
analytical ear that prefers detail, words and names. It is not important to know
which ear is dominant – what is important is that you stimulate both ears simultaneously to strengthen networks to both and not just to the dominant ear.
Binaural (with both ears) hearing is a lifelong gift that promotes ease of learning
and superb communication skills.

BabyGym – Brain and body gym for babies

To do

- Gently massage the earlobes simultaneously, from top to bottom, between the fingers and thumbs to promote the rapid growth of networks between the earlobes and the brain.

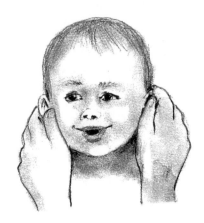

- Massage the shoulder and neck muscles by cradling the head in the palm of your one hand, while making soft circular movements with your fingers from the neck to each shoulder in turn.

- While still cradling the head in the palm of your hand, move the head gently from side to side.

- Use bells, chimes, keys or a rattle and shake it to the left of your baby's head close to the ear. Wait for baby to turn her head towards the sound. Slowly move the sound towards the right ear and wait for baby to follow. It may take weeks for baby to follow, but don't be alarmed or get despondent. Remember that the sound resounded into the ear, which in turn tickled the hair in the ear to change the sound into an electrical impulse that forges its way to the hearing centre of the brain, which sends a message to the head to turn. Forging a network to allow a response takes time.

- Strengthen the neck muscles as this is a prerequisite for good hearing. Tummy time is a must, even if your baby protests a bit. Remember that babies have to adjust their breathing when turned from lying on their backs onto their tummies, which can be quite scary for them. Just make them feel supported but don't give in and return them to lying on their backs. They will soon get used to it. When lying on their tummies babies reflexively start lifting their heads. It is the beginning of a long sequence of events to enable your little one to spell, read and write with ease later.

Physical development

- Should your baby not enjoy tummy time, it is helpful to prop her up on your midsection while lying on your back so that the neck and back-strengthening benefits of tummy time are gained while she is nestled against the warmth of your body: Baby constantly extends her head and neck but always returns to your soft midsection. This strengthens the entire extensor neck and back area without upsetting the child by putting her on her tummy when the neck and back are not yet strong enough to lift easily. At the same time, it is a delightful bonding opportunity for baby and parent. Once baby is strong enough, she will no longer object to tummy time.

- Talk, sing, read and say simple rhymes, even to a tiny baby, as this provides some of the best auditory stimulation a baby can get.
- Play with squeaky toys.
- Play music or activate a musical mobile to expand the range of hearing.
- Exposure to different languages is a good idea as long as the same songs or phrases are repeated. The golden rule for baby gym is repetition, repetition and repetition.

BabyGym – Brain and body gym for babies

WAKING UP THE EYES

The eyes are justifiably said to be the mirror of the soul, since they reflect the person's thoughts, feelings and level of brain activity. Cloudy eyes may indicate headaches or a state of confusion, while bright and shiny eyes generally reflect happiness and confidence.

Did you know
the eyes are important indicators of what is happening in the brain, because the eyes are the only part of the brain that we can see?

Have you noticed how bright and shiny some people's eyes are? It is often an indication of intelligence and brain activity. Dull and lifeless eyes may indicate that the brain is still like a dense forest with only a few forged pathways, which means there is hope for growth and development. In a way it is as though the neurochemical pathways light up the brain and the eyes. Of course, dull eyes could also indicate illness, eyestrain or inadequate sleep!

The eyes are crucial to all later academic reading and writing, but are also the last sense to develop fully. It is said that the eyes are only able to read with ease on a two-dimensional plane (books, computers and electronic games) at the age of seven. Emphasis on paperwork, workbooks and reading before the eyes have matured sufficiently may impact negatively in the long term.

Because the eyes are so close to the brain, one would expect the networks to form quickly. It takes the eyes more or less seven years to develop because their movements are controlled by some of the most intricate muscles. These

Physical development

intricate muscles take years to develop fully because gross (big) muscles develop first and then the smaller muscles for fine muscle control. The core muscles (abdominals) in the tummy are the gross muscles helping the eyes to move!

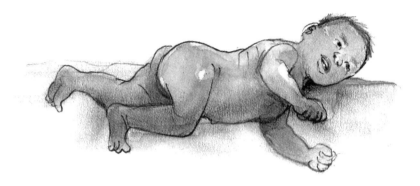

The body follows the eyes

Have you noticed how babies turn their whole bodies when they want to use their eyes to follow you walking across the room? Initially the baby's whole body is involved in controlling the eyes. It's the links teaming up your baby's inner eye muscles with the core muscles in her tummy and back that allow the baby to follow with her eyes. Optometrists often recommend a back and stomach muscle exercise programme to improve eyesight for this very same reason. Babies who are constantly supported by reclining chairs, push chairs, walking rings, pillows or otherwise restrained in their movements do not have the freedom to develop their core muscles. Unsupported rug-time is crucial for free movement, which stimulates core muscle development.

The complex functioning of the eyes may be illustrated by likening the interaction between the eyes and the brain to that between a computer mouse and computer software. When the eyes turn, they access different programmes or parts of the brain.

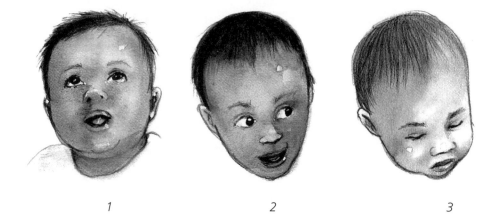

1. When the eyes turn upwards they 'click on the buttons' to access vision.
2. When the eyes turn sideways towards the ears, they click the buttons to access hearing.
3. When the eyes turn downward, they click on the buttons to access awareness of the near senses (self-talk and feelings).

When waking up the eyes, it is important to stimulate all three visual planes to the left and to the right to ensure that all the necessary circuitry develops optimally.

As is the case with the ears, every baby is born with a dominant eye. The dominant eye does the focussing and the other eye has a supporting function. The left eye is the creative eye that loves pictures, colours, shapes and the big picture, while the right eye is the analytical eye that loves words, facts and details. Developing both eyes to work together as a team is crucial for spelling, reading, maths and writing, as well as for picking out Mom or Dad's face in a crowd, or spotting a favourite toy. The eyes direct the whole body, and therefore visual stimulation is very important for all later life skills.

Physical development

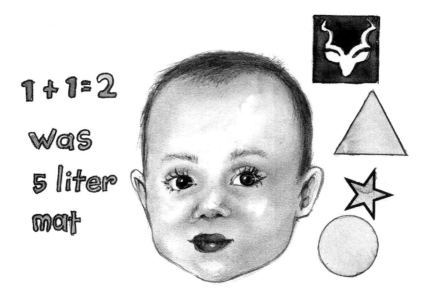

1 + 1 = 2

was

5 liter

mat

To do

- Make eye contact with your baby when you speak to her. Because babies battle to focus soon after birth, bobbing your head while talking to your baby helps her to focus.
- Initially a baby can't see far, so near visual stimulation is necessary. An over-hanging and moving mobile is helpful because it directs your baby's eyes into pushing the buttons for the visual centre in the brain. A versatile mobile on which you can regularly hang new objects is more beneficial than one expensive mobile. It is important to change the objects hanging from the mobile to keep the little one's attention.
- Walk around with your baby and point at, and discuss, objects as though baby understands every word you're saying. Babies are masters at picking up subtle messages from your voice, which enables them to know how to respond. Every time you talk to your baby, you forge a pathway to not only the visual centres, but also to the hearing centres of the brain, which are the basic building blocks of social development.

BabyGym – Brain and body gym for babies

- Let baby lie on your lap facing you. Gently take her hands and pull baby into a sitting position. It is similar to the sit-ups and crunches adults do in the gym. This will strengthen the core muscles that will support eye movements later. Remember to carry this exercise out smoothly because jerky movements won't be beneficial. In the beginning you will do all the work, but gradually baby will start doing some of the work in pulling into a sitting position.

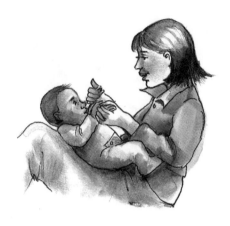

- Put baby flat on her back on a rug. Bend her knees a little and keep the shoulders flat on the rug. Gently rock the knees from side to side to create some flexibility between the top and the bottom of the body. After a few weeks you may notice that baby starts to become familiar with the movements and starts participating actively.

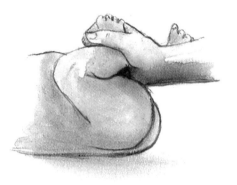

- Play music of your choice and put baby on your lap in a lying or sitting position. Take a little hand in each of yours and pretend that baby is the director of the music. Move the hands simultaneously in opposite directions to stimulate both hands, eyes and parts of the brain at the same time.

Physical development

- Stand in front of a mirror holding baby towards the mirror and talk and gesture with baby's hands.
- Blow bubbles.
- Take a colourful toy in your hand and move it slowly in such a way that baby needs to turn her eyes upwards first, then sideways and, after a while, downwards. This ensures that all the buttons in the brain are being stimulated.

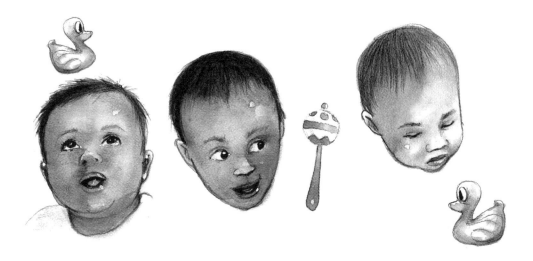

- Games such as peek-a-boo are great for developing neck and eye muscles, as well as visual memory.
- When developing the eye muscles soon after birth, remember to have the objects or toys no further than 30 cm from baby's face to help her to see them easily.

WAKING UP THE NEAR SENSES

The near senses are the ones that help baby to orientate herself in space, to right the body when about to topple over, and to maintain a sense of balance. The development of the near senses starts with a battle against Newton's law of gravity. It is quite natural to rather lie down than stand up, because it requires strength, balance and co-ordination to stand up and resist the pull of gravity. The greater the surface exposed to gravity, the greater the pull. Baby's near senses should be stimulated so she may become more flexible in space while moving towards an upright body posture, in this way minimising the area of the body's surface exposed to gravity.

Movement is the essential ingredient for near-sensory stimulation. The necessity for carrying, swinging, rocking and turning baby around to stimulate the near senses may be demonstrated by comparing the working of the vestibular system to a 'snow globe'. You know those see-through globes depicting a scene and filled with water and 'snow'? When you shake it the snow is disturbed, sifts down and settles after a while. When a person moves, the liquid in the inner ear is disturbed but settles down after a while, leaving you feeling balanced and in control. When the fluid doesn't settle down easily due to infection or poor development, one is left with a feeling of dizziness, disorientation and even nausea. Near senses are important later in life in terms of planning, organisation, resilience and maintaining balance.

Near senses are also involved in muscle control as they instruct muscles to expand or contract, to anticipate weight or not, to move the head to the left or to the right and to shift weight to avoid toppling over. Movement is needed to shake up the fluid in the ear and instruct the muscles how to respond.

To do

- Play with your baby – it is impossible to play without moving.
- Carry your newborn baby in a pouch on your back and on your chest.
- Invest in a rocking chair for the nursery to gently and rhythmically rock baby while feeding or comforting.
- Push baby in a stroller over different types of terrain – paving, tar, gravel – at an incline and down a slope. All these different surfaces stimulate the near senses in a variety of ways.
- When baby is a little older, stimulating the near senses could be Dad's duty, because dads are usually better than moms at playing more physical games. Babies need to wrestle, ride horse on the foot, sit on Dad's back and to be swung gently through the air.

- Any push-bike, tricycle or even a bicycle with training wheels is wonderful for near-sense stimulation. The whole family can join in this activity.
- It is a great idea to obtain a big ball for rolling and later for kicking and throwing. Ball games promote muscle control, motor planning and balance.
- It is also helpful to let baby pull or push a toy.
- Allow lots of rug-time that baby may explore freely.
- Do not let baby sit in a reclining chair or stroller watching TV, as this is **not** conducive to your baby optimising this window of opportunity to discover her own body and its competencies.

BabyGym – Brain and body gym for babies

FOLLOWING THE DEVELOPMENTAL PHASES

If your baby is more relaxed through your touch and gentle massage, and all the senses have been tickled and woken up, the next step is to follow the naturally unfolding developmental phases to strengthen the muscles and co-ordinate the body.

It is fascinating to observe how consistently each developmental stage or milestone emerges from the previous one, and how development in all children proceeds according to the same basic laws, despite individual, ethnic and gender differences. These milestones are the basic building blocks of all learning later in school. It works a little like the layers of an onion – each developmental phase develops a layer of the brain and body that supports the next layer. These layers develop from the most basic muscle groups to the most sophisticated and intricate muscle groups. Think about the skill needed to move your arm, compared to the skill needed to thread a needle. Moving an arm requires strength and purpose, but threading a needle needs strength, purpose, stability, eye-teaming skills, balance and fine muscle control.

> Developmental phases of the brain and body may be compared to the layers of an onion.

The sequence of the development of the layers is crucial to optimal functioning. You sometimes find a brown ring in the middle of an otherwise juicy and healthy onion, and to avoid forming a similar brown ring in baby's development the phases need to follow in sequence.

The following description of some of the stages in healthy whole-brain and body development by no means professes to be comprehensive – at the back of the book (p. 117) you will find a list of books that describe these phases in depth. In *BabyGym* the description of the phases is limited to what you need

Physical development

to know for drawing the links between the developmental phases and their relevance to whole-brain learning.

Did you know
a typical baby tends to follow a known developmental sequence that starts at birth in a head-to-toe progression?

The muscles and networks around the head are the first to develop as they are closer to the branching neurons in the brain, and therefore, the networks are shorter and easier to grow compared to networks that have to reach the toes. Now it is easier to understand why it takes a baby many months to learn to walk!

Baby gestures like squirming, reaching, touching and tasting help the formation and organisation of networks between body parts that later control thinking processes, such as concentration, comprehension, creative problem-solving and memory. These seemingly pointless repeated body actions effectively sculpt the brain into a complex work of art, while connecting all the neurochemical branches into one efficient processor of information.

A playing, moving, gurgling baby is hard at work.

BabyGym – Brain and body gym for babies

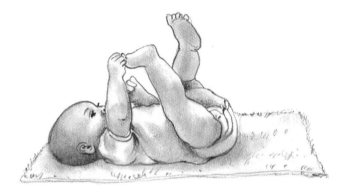

When baby is lying unhampered on the rug, his movements may appear very natural and easy to Mom and Dad, but for the baby most movements are new and difficult. To relate to the challenges a baby is faced with, think of a time when you learned to ski, ice-skate or rock-climb. Even though you were strong, fit and well co-ordinated, it took a lot of repetition to build the strength and agility to become competent at these exploits.

Parents are often overheard saying proudly: "**My** child walked at nine months." "**My** child sat at four months." "**My** child was potty trained at eighteen months." The **speed** of your child's progression is not what is important – faster is not better, quality is the important factor. The more time children spend naturally repeating their actions and games during each developmental phase, the better the chances that the networks will branch out and interconnect extensively. Every moment spent in stimulating your baby with real and concrete objects that he can taste, touch, smell, see and hear and every rug-time moment exploring movement freely is an opportunity to gain experience and build networks. The complexity of the developing networks creates a stable base for baby to later build concepts needed for reasoning on an abstract level when, for instance, discovering symbols and doing maths.

Supports like reclining chairs, donut cushions, walking rings, and strollers are handy when you need your hands free for a little while, but they restrict

Physical development

natural movement and hence your baby's ability to learn. Do you remember that development is the result of the inborn need to be somebody and to be accepted by others? And that these two needs evoke enthusiasm that releases neurochemicals to form new networks? When a baby lies on his tummy and struggles to lift his head, he may moan a little. It is like when you carry heavy shopping bags – you moan a little, but it has to be done. It is through lying on the tummy and raising the head that baby develops the crucial link between core muscles and the eye muscles – it is the start of literacy networks.

Experience is the teacher and **stimulation** the method.

From the moment of birth, informal education starts, but, according to Mark Twain, for some children education is not as sudden as a massacre, but it is more deadly in the long run.

Educating, stimulating and developing your baby's potential is not about forcing and pushing to accomplish certain outputs at specific times. It is about giving your baby the space, stimulation and time to unfold, while noting the milestones as they are reached as beacons of natural progress. The most appropriate sequence of development is from gross-motor (big muscles controlling body, head and limbs for large motor movement, such as standing and walking) to fine-motor (smaller muscles controlling more precise actions like lip, finger, toe and eye movements). Motor skill determines the level of motor control and integration, which later affects the child's ability to concentrate, delay gratification (wait), plan and carry out tasks to completion.

Generally, soon after birth a baby will start opening his eyes for a little while, notice the light and sounds, and curiously look from side to side, developing the strength and co-ordination in the

BabyGym – Brain and body gym for babies

neck and upper-back muscles. At about two months of age, baby will be able to hold his head up and look around. After much practice, baby will raise both legs while lying flat on his back, simultaneously developing the core muscles while nearly touching his head with his toes at times! Between three to four months a baby starts rolling over to reach a favourite toy just out of reach. When placed in a sitting position, around six months of age, baby will start stabilising himself by using both hands for support. Within a month or two baby can get into and out of a sitting position unaided and will also start playing with a toy while in a sitting position.

This marks celebration time! Just think about the amount of skill involved in being able to hold the head and body up, balance to not topple over, hand-eye co-ordination to spot and grasp a toy, and eye-mouth co-ordination to explore a toy with the mouth. And to think just a few months ago baby was still a scrunched-up, floppy, and fully dependent little human being!

During rug-time, baby starts inching around on his tummy, kicking and waving his arms. After a while he discovers the all-fours position and rocks forwards and backwards till all of a sudden

Physical development

he starts to crawl. Generally, by his first birthday, baby has figured out how to pull himself up into a standing position, cruise along the furniture and maybe even take a few steps alone. Research indicates that only 60% of all children venture a step or two alone by their first birthday. It's only two or three months later that most babies are qualified to be called Homo sapiens (modern man who walks upright).

DISCOVERING AND MASTERING THE BODY THROUGH GROSS-MOTOR MOVEMENT

Gross-motor developmental phases and sequence of milestones include:
- Head control
- Hip flexion and trunk rotation
- Rolling
- Grasping
- Sitting
- Crawling
- Standing, cruising and walking.

> The sequence and the duration of the developmental phases hold the key to all future performance.

Some of these developmental phases, and their corresponding actions, can start simultaneously. The lifting of the head and the grasping reflex may, for instance, start at the same time, but critical readiness time to complete and inhibit those reflexes will differ. Critical readiness time is the time when the reflex has completed its job of stimulating a specific area of development through repetition of the same activities, such as strengthening the neck muscles by lifting the head over and over. Most babies are able to hold the head up at 14 weeks (critical readiness time for neck control), but are able to voluntarily grasp a toy only at 26 weeks (critical readiness time for the grasping reflex).

A word of caution – the times within which milestones are reached are by no means exactly the same for every baby and are therefore given here within a timeframe followed by the words *or so*. The duration in weeks or months indicated in *BabyGym* is based on the average trends observed and documented by scientific research.

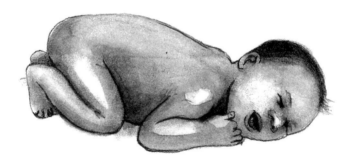

HEAD CONTROL

Head control is the first movement a baby conquers and is necessary for attaining other movement skills such as sitting, crawling and walking. Head control requires the muscles that bend and extend to strengthen and co-ordinate. Babies are born 'bent' to fit in the womb and through repeatedly attempting to lift the head, they straighten the muscles and the spine.

Physical development

To develop head control, babies are generally reflexively motivated to turn their heads in an attempt to locate a sound or look around. When a newborn baby is lying down, the head normally lies to the side, and only after a few weeks can baby hold his head in mid-position (midfield). When you try to pull a newborn baby up by his hands into a sitting position, the head naturally falls back.

Strengthening the neck and back muscles through on-tummy rug-time also utilises the near senses to precisely register the position of the head in relationship to the body. Via the neurochemical branches, the brain then sends a message to the corresponding muscles to adjust the head till it is upright. The head is the spirit level (like a ruler with a bubble in the middle used to show if a surface is straight) of the body.

To do

- Place baby on his back on your lap. Place both your hands behind his shoulders and provide as much support as is needed to prevent the head from dropping back. If baby's neck is very floppy, rather place your hands behind his neck and, over time, move your hands towards the shoulders as the head control improves. Slowly raise baby towards you into a sitting position. Slowly release the pressure and allow baby to relax back against your lap. Repeat a few times.

- When baby is a little stronger you can raise him from your lap into a sitting position by allowing the little hands to grasp your fingers. Ensure that you have a solid grip to avoid baby dropping back all of a sudden.

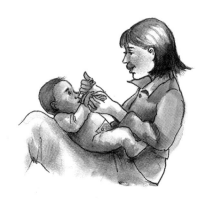

BabyGym — Brain and body gym for babies

- Shake a rattle or keys to encourage head turning.
- Gently stroke baby's cheek with a variety of soft textures, like a washcloth, soft toy or cotton wool to encourage head turning. Stimulate the left and the right cheek.
- Approach your baby from both sides to encourage head turning to both the left and the right. If you notice a preference for turning to one side only, approach baby from the other side more often. Balance and flexibility in movement is the key to optimal head control.
- If your baby shows very little ability to turn or lift his head, gently massage both ears simultaneously from the top to the bottom of the earlobe. This action will tickle the near senses and wake them up to control the head. Now hold his head gently in your hand and slowly turn it from side to side, also gently push the head downwards and then lift it. Repeat often.

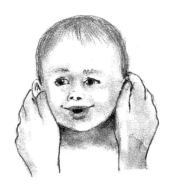

- Sit on the floor with your knees slightly raised and place baby on your lap. Gently rock from side to side, and forwards and backwards, allowing baby the opportunity to keep his head upright.

The benefits

Head control provides baby with a new perspective on his surroundings and promotes eye control.

HIP FLEXION AND TRUNK ROTATION

Hip flexion starts developing simultaneously to baby learning to control his head. Hip flexion is best noticed from birth onwards when a baby lies on his back kicking vigorously and unhampered with both legs. The need for kicking space is normally felt by Mom while baby is still *in utero*. Now that he has the space to kick, baby is discovering the range of motion his hips allow. The legs tirelessly bend and straighten all the time, extending their range of movement until sufficient strength and control is gained to hold the legs up for a while.

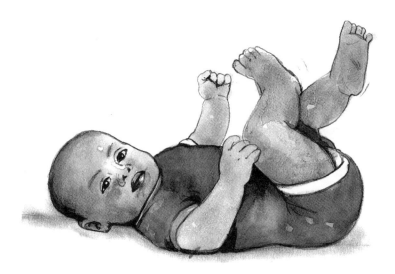

Hip flexion

Hip flexion without trunk rotation would not prepare the baby to roll, sit, crawl or walk. Trunk rotation is a movement that occurs along the trunk of the body, between the hips and the shoulders. Until the trunk can rotate, the baby stays immobile. Trunk rotation enables the baby to change position and is therefore one step closer to mobility.

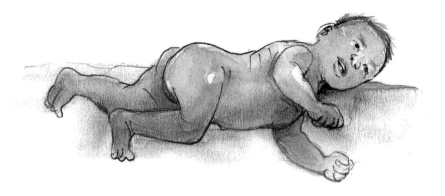

Trunk rotation

Have you noticed how many teenagers can't sit or stand upright without supporting themselves on an arm or leaning against something? This is due to underdeveloped core muscles, hip flexion and trunk rotation. When not lying down, the brain will always pay attention to keeping the body as upright as possible to minimise the pull of gravity. Slouching, or sitting upright with support, keeps teenagers' brains occupied with the fight against gravity instead of paying attention in class. The child then needs to work harder to concentrate, which is exhausting and leads to attention deficit and low energy levels.

To do

- Put baby on your lap or the rug and take his ankles in your hands. Push the ankles upwards, one at a time, to bend the knees one after the other – thus you have a pedalling action. Move the legs slowly as though going up a hill and then fast as though going downhill. Create a story while doing the actions, to link listening skills to gross-motor movement.

Physical development

- While baby's still on his back, take his left hand and gently bring it closer (flex it) to the right knee until it touches. Move the leg and arm apart till they are extended, and then take the right hand and do the same with the left leg. You may find it takes a while to create a smooth movement, but work with baby – gently moving while waiting for baby to follow.

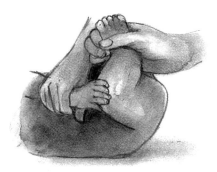

- Still flat on the back, take baby's feet in one hand and push them up gently to bend the knees. With gentle pressure from the other hand, keep the shoulders flat while rocking the legs from side to side. Once there is more flexibility in the trunk and hip, you can draw big circles with baby's knees to extend the range of movement. Rotate to the left and to the right.

- Sit baby down on your lap and hold him by the hips while rocking him forwards and backwards, left and right, up and down, to strengthen and link the sense of balance to trunk rotation and hip flexion.

ROLLING

Rolling over is the natural next step in the progression of baby discovering his body and what it can do. The ability to roll smoothly from back to tummy, and tummy to back, requires some degree of head control and trunk rotation.

Rolling is the first movement that allows a baby to be mobile. Babies take delight in the sensation of moving their bodies about through rolling. Watch a

BabyGym – Brain and body gym for babies

baby rolling over and you would note an apparent preference for rolling more to the one side than to the other. It is said that a baby tends to roll away from its dominant brain hemisphere (left or right) and needs to be guided to roll both ways – to the left and the right. A baby is born with a dominant brain side, but to ensure whole-brain development, both sides of the brain need to be stimulated.

To do

- Start off with lots of rug-time. Place baby on his back and allow him to explore freely.
- After a while, turn baby over onto his tummy and again let him explore freely. Place a colourful object within his range of vision but out of reach. Seeing the object will stimulate the need to move towards it. Lying on his tummy helps baby to develop the ability to shift weight from side to side and to bear his own weight as he begins to prop himself up on his forearms.

- If your baby finds it difficult to roll, you can help him roll until sufficient muscle memory has been created. Then roll baby onto his side and let him complete the rolling process on his own. Repeat for a few days until baby starts doing it by himself. Make sure your baby is not wearing restrictive clothing as this will inhibit movement.

Physical development

GRASPING

Think of what happens when one or both of your hands is injured – you are no longer able to do the most mundane of tasks, such as bathing, dressing, eating with a knife and fork, gesturing while talking, or working on the computer. Without touch, the weight, temperature and texture of an object can no longer be judged. Thus hands are involved with most daily activities, perception and communication, and therefore exceptionally important for thinking, independence, self-reliance and for building relationships with others.

BabyGym – Brain and body gym for babies

A baby is born with tiny, closed fists and can neither voluntarily open the fists nor stretch an arm in a specific direction. The involuntary grasping reflex, which accounts for the clenched fists, disappears within two months and only then does the development of actual grasping become possible.

Between the second and fourth months, baby discovers his hands and seems to be fascinated by them as he rotates them close to the eyes. At four months baby can bring his half-open hands together in the direction of an object to hold it. More or less in the sixth month, baby can grasp an object accurately, hold it firmly and even pass it from one hand to the other.

Holding on does not mean he can let go! Baby needs to learn how to voluntarily let go of an object by dropping it. Only by the ninth month can a baby

Physical development

drop a toy by choice and only by his first birthday can he place a toy in a container or in Dad's hand.

Grasping also has to progress from whole-hand to pincer-grip control, which later assists the baby in holding a writing implement and being able to write. Stretching the thumb and positioning it opposite the rest of the hand to form a pair of tweezers requires planning and fine-motor control. This is the beginning of finger control, which is indispensable for all fine-motor skills. Pincer grip is a prerequisite for eating, dressing, all block building, pegboard activities, puzzle building and eventually drawing, and later, writing skills.

Did you know
that the hands and the language centres of the brain are part of the same neural pathway? This means that when babies develop their grasp and fine motor control, they are also developing their language abilities.

To do

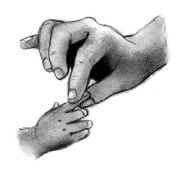

- Begin with a simple hand massage. Use your thumb to softly unfold the hand from the wrist to the tip of each finger individually. Rub the tips of the fingers so the brain can register up to where it needs to grow branches.
- Use your index finger and gently stroke the palms of baby's hands – the fingers will automatically clutch, unfold and stroke. Always remember to stimulate both hands.

BabyGym – Brain and body gym for babies

- Tease the hands with a solid object small enough to fit in the palm of the hand but too big to fit in the mouth. The handle of a rattle or a teething ring works well. When the hand closes around it, gently pull it out of the hand. Repeat with many different textures and sizes.
- Play finger games with your little one or say finger rhymes, such as *This little piggy went to market*, touching each finger as you go along.
- Place objects close enough to baby that he may explore them. It is better to put out only one or two toys at a time than to tip the whole toy box. Because baby's vision is not sufficiently developed yet, he gets overwhelmed and loses interest.
- During rug-time, also try to avoid using a multicoloured, patterned rug, as baby finds it difficult to distinguish toys from the rug.
- Give baby everyday articles such as a hairbrush, facecloth (a damp facecloth on a hot day ensures minutes of fun) and measuring spoons to touch and explore, and name each article as you pass it. Vary the textures by using articles made from different materials such as metal, plastic, wood and fabric.
- Teach baby to clap hands and wave goodbye. Be patient – it takes a long time. Take one of baby's hands and sway it in a waving motion. Name the action. Take baby's hands and clap them together gently. This helps baby to build muscle memory and promotes co-ordination.
- Demonstrate by dropping toys or everyday objects, then overlap baby's hand with yours and pick up a toy. Purposely drop it. Respond with enthusiasm!

Towards the end of the first year a plastic container or basket (with a big opening), filled with toys or blocks can keep your little one happily occupied for a long time by taking out toys and dropping them back in.

Once baby has mastered the art of emptying and filling a basket, a container with openings for differently shaped blocks comes in handy. Start off by finding the hole for the circle. Put the circle in and take it out. Repeat this action till baby can do it on his own and then add another simple shape.

Physical development

Did you know
the average parent tends to say "no" or "don't" eighteen times
to each "well done"?

Positive feedback reinforces the baby's actions and increases baby's level of enthusiasm, which stimulates the growth of neurochemical networks. Positive reinforcement and praise speeds up the learning process.

BabyGym – Brain and body gym for babies

SITTING

The ability to maintain a sitting position requires baby to have sufficient muscle strength to resist the pull of gravity. Baby also needs a well-developed sense of balance and protective responses in the forward, backward and side-to-side directions. Protective responses are responses that keep babies safe and protect them from getting hurt, as when they put their hands out to prevent them from toppling over. If baby has muscle tightness in the hips and legs, or a weakness in the trunk or neck muscles, sitting is not easy. Go back a step or two and strengthen neck muscles and trunk rotation first.

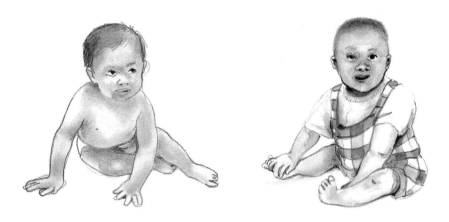

Initially baby sits by supporting himself with both hands in front of him. As balance and upright posture improve, he comes to rely on his near senses to instruct the hand to move to the side to prevent him from falling over. After much practice the baby can hold himself up without using his hands for balance.

To do

- Place baby on a rug in a sitting position and sit down behind him to provide support. Spread his legs apart to create a stable base. Place a colourful toy in front of baby to encourage him to prop himself up on both hands while

Physical development

leaning forward. If baby can't put both hands on the rug, help by placing both his hands on the rug and pushing him forward a little that he may experience the feel of weight on his hands and arms. Rock baby gently forward to experience the propping position.

- Once baby can sit propped forward, you want to encourage side-to-side balance by placing a toy beside him. Place baby's hand near the toy and help him shift his weight onto that hand to free the other hand to reach for the toy. Repeat this activity to the left and to the right.

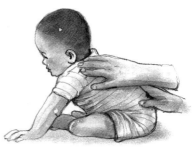

- Rolling a smallish foam ball towards your baby will improve his sitting skills.
- Playing with cars, trucks or any toy on wheels strengthens core muscle stability. Boys *and* girls can play with cars.
- Nappy, bath or dressing times may be turned into times for practising sitting.
- Baby should be sitting quite securely by ten months or so.
- Once baby sits comfortably and securely, get Dad to challenge baby by gently pushing him backwards to trigger the righting reflexes. Do the same forward, and towards the sides.

Did you know
as rolling develops the left and the right side of the brain, so crawling integrates the two sides to work together as a team?

BabyGym – Brain and body gym for babies

CRAWLING

Crawling organises the non-thinking areas of the central nervous system. These important areas in the brain form the foundation upon which learning and development are constructed. When these areas develop well, a solid foundation for learning, growing and glowing occurs naturally and easily. If this area lacks development, confused, unfocused and disorganised learning, as well as difficulties in knowing the left from the right, can occur.

This is probably one of the most important phases in the development of babies as it promotes gross and fine-motor control, strengthens the near and far senses, develops neural pathways and increases the formation of myelin around each nerve fibre. Do not hurry your child through this phase as every baby needs to crawl an average of 50 000 times before he is ready to move on to the next developmental stage.

Crawling starts with head control, followed by trunk rotation and hip flexion. Because sitting promotes propping the body up with both hands it is also an important aspect in the run-up to crawling. Crawling without long periods of rug-time is impossible.

Physical development

As soon as baby can lie on his tummy and prop himself up on his hands, he is getting ready to crawl. When the hands and arms can take the body weight and the head and chest are raised, baby starts making movements similar to a frog swimming. Because it is an uncomfortable posture, the brain comes to the rescue by instructing the knees to help support the body weight. Babies learn through action, and being stationary on hands and knees is not active enough, so by about the eighth month, a baby will start rocking on all fours. They rock to try out their balancing reactions to be sure they have mastered this posture before they start moving forward.

Baby will extend his range of rocking till one of the hands moves reflexively forward to prevent him from falling flat on his face. This small success gets repeated until a few weeks later when he can crawl effortlessly and quickly on all fours. Baby-proofing the environment now becomes crucial. Crawling is like one's first trip overseas – the whole world is opened up all of a sudden: It is bigger, looks different and poses lots of stimulation and new experiences! Dresses, although they look pretty, bunch around the knees and prevent forward movement. Also, leaving the baby's knees uncovered can make crawling painful so make sure your baby is wearing comfortable and protective clothing.

Crawling on all fours offers thorough exercise for the complete muscular system. The balancing reactions, and left-right co-ordination stimulated by crawling are prerequisites for walking a little later, while the shoulder girdle is stabilised as the basis for fine-motor (hand) control.

BabyGym – Brain and body gym for babies

To do

- Allow plenty of rug-time on the tummy.
- Place toys or a treat just out of reach to stimulate the desire to be mobile.
- Toys with wheels naturally invite more movement and are appropriate for girls and boys.
- If your baby shows no sign of start-  ing or wanting to crawl, fold a tea towel or towel nappy into a rectangle. Place the rectangle on the floor and place baby on his tummy on the folded cloth with its ends sticking out on both sides of baby. Pull the ends upwards and baby's body will automatically rise into an all-fours position. Gently rock baby forwards and backwards. Do this daily till baby starts moving into the crawling position of his own accord.
- If baby rocks but doesn't move forward, sit in front of baby and encourage him to come to you. Sit close enough that one or two movements will land baby in your arms. Remember to be generous with words of encouragement and major praise when this task is mastered. The baby may feel very isolated on the floor so get down there and join him.
- Build a simple obstacle course for baby to crawl under chairs, over cushions and through your legs.
- Play with a ball and with friction toys that run out of motion and need to be recovered.
- Give simple instructions to go and fetch a nappy or a toy.
- Avoid walking rings and other equipment that promote an upright posture before baby has crawled. This could damage their skeletal development and cause problems later on in life.

Physical development

STANDING, CRUISING AND WALKING

Crawling around has given baby a new perspective on the environment, and as soon as the thrill of crawling starts to wane, baby's natural curiosity takes over again. Baby now has the strength, balance and co-ordination to pull himself up into a standing position, and often gets alarmed by his own height when trying to lower himself. This new perspective fascinates the baby so much, that he sometimes forgets how to sit down again!

As your baby pulls himself onto his feet, he gains additional strength and control in his trunk and leg muscles. Soon baby is confident enough to start cruising sideways around the furniture. Baby simply loves holding on to Mom or Dad's hands while taking his first step forward. The hips tend to be overextended and the legs stiff, but sheer enthusiasm still propels baby forward. Much repetition and encouragement later, the baby who was at one moment still cruising along the furniture, suddenly develops the necessary neurochemical connections and takes his first unaided step.

Physical development

To do

- Make the environment babysafe. Once a baby starts moving there is no stopping it.
- Ensure there is not a single tablecloth within reach, as baby may mistake it for a stable object and try to pull himself up by it.
- To make the pulling-up phase easier, provide a low obstacle on which a baby can kneel and then pull up.
- If baby still doesn't pull himself up, place him in a kneeling position in front of the obstacle. Raise the one knee and put the foot flat down on the ground. Gently lift baby in such a way that he will shift his weight onto the foot. Slowly raise baby into an upright position. Repeat a few times over a couple of days.

- You can also put baby on his knees facing you and let him grab your hands. Gently pull baby into a standing position. As baby develops more strength, allow him to do most of the work.
- Push toys, kiddie strollers and boxes provide superb opportunities to practise walking while comforting baby with the idea that he is still being supported.

BabyGym – Brain and body gym for babies

Too early for fine motor control

BabyGym concentrates on babyhood (birth to two years), when the gross motor skills are developed. It is inadvisable to pay premature attention to fine motor control and co-ordination before the gross motor muscles are strong and co-ordinated. *BabyGym* wants to help caregivers to establish a sound foundation at the gross motor level.

Physical development

Social development

I AM NOT ALONE – THE WORLD IS FULL OF PEOPLE AND THINGS

The second window of opportunity for development occurs when your baby discovers other people and the world. Soon afterwards, baby also discovers her feelings and emotions about people and the world. Feelings and emotions are messengers that tell the head what the heart is feeling. These emotional messengers are activated when baby starts relating to other people and the world, and therefore emotional and social development occur concurrently.

Do you still remember that the two driving forces that propel a child to learn and grow are the need to be somebody and the need to be accepted? **Physical development** is a step towards being somebody (an independent individual), and the need to make contact and be accepted by others is a step towards **social and emotional development**.

REACHING OUT

Like a relocating adult needs a map to explore a new environment, a baby needs a map and pointers on how to reach out and make contact. Social development starts from the moment of conception. The baby unconsciously starts communicating with Mom by making her feel queasy or just 'different'. Mom's near senses pick up the baby's presence in the womb and the moment Mom's near senses start telling her about baby's presence, communication and social

BabyGym – Brain and body gym for babies

development begins! If Mom is ecstatic about baby's presence, baby experiences Mom's reaction as social acceptance. If baby has arrived at an inopportune time, baby may have her first experience of social rejection.

Even though baby is aware of Mom's reactions, mood and general state of being, the critical time for emotional and social development opens up around baby's fourteenth month. At that age, baby has physically developed sufficiently to be independent – she knows how to get around by crawling and maybe even walking. She can move objects around and can even start tugging at her nappy or clothes when she wants to be changed. Baby also knows how to communicate when she wants to be fed, is thirsty or wants to be comforted, and whom to 'talk' to to have these needs met. Baby has thus realised that she has to rely on other people to be happy and have her needs met. Once baby realises she needs others to make things happen, she has entered the window of opportunity for social development.

Babies of working parents in particular are often in day care by this age, and this is where day mothers and other caregivers are often substitutes for parents for the larger part of the baby's waking hours. If you are a caregiver, your charge/charges will benefit immensely from the activities described on the following pages. As a parent it could be valuable to point this out to other people caring for your child.

Did you know
it is only during interaction with humans that a child becomes
a human being?

Social development without emotional and language development is impossible. To illustrate this point, many case studies have been recorded where children were abandoned and raised by animals and where, even though the children looked like humans, their behaviour, means of communication and ability to connect emotionally resembled animal behaviour.

As a result of baby's need to make contact with others and her environment, a new growth spurt in the relationship-building part of the brain (called the limbic system) is triggered, which heralds social development. Because baby wants to reach out to, and get in touch with, people and her surroundings, the brain starts growing neurochemical branches between the senses, the feeling and thinking/talking parts of the brain, and the mouth, hands and feet. These branches develop through repetition driven by the need to be accepted.

Social, language and emotional development happen simultaneously, but for the sake of clarity will be discussed separately. Because emotions are the heart's way of communicating to the head what is important and what is not, the head can only make sense of the heart's message if it has the words with which to think.

> ### Did you know
> without words there is no rational thinking?

Any emotion, without the words to make sense of the particular emotion's message and the ability to communicate it to others, leads to frustration and emotional outbursts. Temper tantrums may therefore be seen as an expression of a need arising from an intense emotion without the ability to verbalise the true nature of the feeling. The so-called terrible twos mark the next stage of your baby's development – social, emotional and language development. While the window of opportunity for language development is between fourteen months and four years, it is most noticeable at two years – time to celebrate!

BabyGym – Brain and body gym for babies

But isn't it confusing that even though baby is now supposed to learn how to be socially acceptable, she throws one socially unacceptable temper tantrum after the other? For most people, transition from one phase to the next tends to be difficult and so it is in the case of a baby. Learning to be acceptable implies also learning about what is unacceptable, but at that age the dividing line between what is acceptable and what's not, is faint. The dividing line needs to become clear and the way parents normally define that is by saying *no* and *yes*. As mentioned earlier, research has indicated that parents tend to give negative feedback by saying *no* eighteen times for every single positive reinforcement, often expressed by *yes*.

Social development

At the age of two, baby has learned the word *no* and uses it with regularity because she has heard it numerous times, said with intensity and emphasis. Mom and Dad say *no* to fence in and keep safe by setting boundaries. Because baby can now walk and explore and has learned to use a few (but only a few) basic words, she tries to model Mom and Dad in setting boundaries. A baby's boundaries are not like parents' boundaries about safety; they are about asserting herself and hence the second favourite word, *self*. When the baby says *self*, she means, "I want to do it myself". *Self* is a cry for freedom and independence.

A major difficulty with emotional and social development, therefore, lies in the contradiction between baby's need to be accepted and the way she goes about it. The baby's behaviour doesn't just happen, it is the result of physical development (that's why they kick and scream so effectively) and the ability to neurochemically connect the feeling heart and the thinking head. Just as baby had to strengthen the leg and back muscles for months before she could stand up, the parts of the brain that control behaviour depend on the development of emotions and vocabulary.

The development of emotions and vocabulary naturally progresses when a child feels socially accepted …

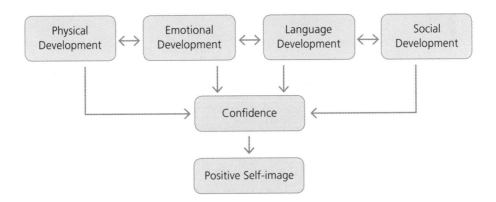

BabyGym – Brain and body gym for babies

A baby learns to be human through her interaction and relationships with others. A newborn baby's experience of the warm softness of Mom's skin and her loving touch, lays the foundation for all baby's later relationships. It is the gentle rocking, talking and stroking of baby's skin during feeding, bathing and changing times that communicate your acceptance to your baby. Baby's first awareness of others is through touch and sound and that is why it is also so important for Dad to hold, touch and talk to baby, otherwise he is a stranger.

In baby's second month she begins to perceive the human face. It is now that the first real smile appears as an expression of happiness and comfort. It is your baby's way of saying, "Thank you, please do some more"!

At about month six or so, baby starts recognising family members and caregivers and distinguishes them from other people. Baby now becomes more selective about whom she smiles at and who may pick her up. This natural reserve or shyness becomes more apparent towards baby's first birthday. This marks another important landmark in baby's life as it builds the foundation for long-term loving relationships and caution towards strangers.

Social development

Also at around month six, babies actively start making contact with their favourite people. Baby no longer just responds to others, she now starts initiating contact with others by calling out, extending the arms to be picked up and wants to play loving games like peek-a-boo.

Dad and baby

During the same period baby follows every move of Mom and Dad that she may learn from them. Baby also starts imitating Mom and Dad's speech and it is at this stage that simple repetitive sounds such as *ma-ma*, *da-da*, and *ta-ta* emerge. At the end of baby's first year, Mom, Dad and baby have built a rich

BabyGym – Brain and body gym for babies

repertoire of communication possibilities that makes baby instinctively aware that she is loved and accepted. It is from this secure and warm 'nest', developed over time, that baby ventures forth to expand her social contacts and social acceptability.

How to stimulate social development
- Talk to baby from the moment she is born – explain what you're doing while performing routine tasks like bathing, clothing and feeding.
- Make and maintain eye contact; it creates a feeling of acceptance.
- Use gentle stroking and touch baby often.
- Rocking baby creates a sense of oneness and acceptance, and hence it is always good to have a rocking chair in the nursery.
- Encourage Dad to often hold, cuddle and talk to baby.
- Tickle baby gently and repeat silly rhymes; laughter fosters reciprocal interactions with others, which promotes social development.

Social development

- Smile and show pleasure.
- Play peek-a-boo.
- Pick babies up when they reach out with their arms – as often as is practical.
- As baby is nearing her first birthday, allow self-feeding.
- Show pride in, and pleasure at, accomplishments.
- Encourage baby to follow instructions, for example while dressing baby say, "Put your foot in here." "Where is your hand?"
- Mirror-time – allow baby to spend time in front of a mirror. Babies love watching the baby in the mirror and talking to it.

BabyGym – Brain and body gym for babies

Emotional development

I HAVE A HEART FULL OF FEELINGS AND EMOTIONS

The window of opportunity for emotional development is between fourteen months and four years. Social development pre-empts emotional development, because emotions are the body's way of letting baby know if he likes the interaction with a person or the environment or not, and also whether or not something is important. Do you remember that all learning is based on experience? Emotions interpret those experiences – they say, "Yes, it was good, must do it again" or, "No, that was yuk!"

> ### Did you know
> emotions are energy in motion?

Because emotions have the ability to mobilise a person, they create action and movement – they propel one forward. Emotions don't only propel forward, they are also crucial ingredients in the creation of memories. If there is no emotional reaction (good or bad, positive or negative) the brain thinks, "Oh, this is not important, I do not need to store the experience in memory." On the other hand,

BabyGym – Brain and body gym for babies

if an experience evokes an intense emotion, the brain reads the heart's message as, "**High priority**, experience needs to be saved for later use". The moment a memory has been saved for later use, learning has taken place! Emotional development in a baby is therefore important and impacts right throughout life because emotional development enables people to connect with other people and is a crucial ingredient in motivation, memory and learning.

Babies are not born with a range of emotions – they need to develop their emotional repertoire. Unfortunately, emotional development has been taken for granted in the past, which has resulted in adults finding it difficult to build long-term and loving relationships. The roots of mature, adult relationships are found in the emotional development of the baby.

Did you know
research by John Bowlby has indicated that "the lack of personal attention in the early years of childhood leads to disorders in social development, inadequate interactions with other people, even leading to unsociability, prostitution and criminality"?

Luckily, as long as there is life there is hope for those who did not receive adequate love and acceptance – many articles, books and workshops have seen the light on EQ (Emotional Intelligence) to enhance emotional development and thus ensure loving long-term relationships. (See bibliography on page 117 for books on EQ.)

Emotional development

HOW DOES A BABY DEVELOP EMOTIONALLY?

As with physical and social development, emotional development requires experience, time and positive feedback. Every time baby does something well, reinforce the behaviour by clapping hands, smiling, and telling baby just what an absolute genius he is. When a newborn baby raises his head, you acknowledge the behaviour, every time baby takes the nipple gently you acknowledge it, every time baby attempts to focus on your face with both eyes you acknowledge it. Every step of each developmental phase is like a job well done that deserves a promotion – celebrate it!

Even though a baby doesn't understand all the words you use to express your wonder and awe at his brilliance, he understands the glow in your eyes and the gentleness in your voice and touch. As is the case with your baby – your body language does the talking.

BabyGym – Brain and body gym for babies

How to stimulate emotional development:

- Stick to a routine – routine creates a sense of safety and security.
- Introduce, and repeat, simple short rhymes from early on.
- Tell or read stories with loads of inflection and dramatisation.
- Play simple games, such as tap the mobile and watch it move, turn on the light switch and marvel at the light, roll a ball or clap hands.
- Show joy when progress is made.
- Give loads of encouragement.
- Say what you are feeling: "You make me happy." "I am proud of you." "I am feeling tired." "What you did made me sad."
- Be honest in your reactions.
- Be consistent.

Emotional development

Cognitive development

I LEARN ABOUT THINKING, NAMES AND WORDS

Names and words are the symbols of thought. Language is a learned code that enables people to express wants and needs and to communicate. It starts off as simple sounds and culminates in writing and reading in later years.

Baby's ability to talk and interact develops gradually through interaction with people and the environment. Language is the natural progression from the sense of vibration and rhythm *in utero*, to tone and hearing in the baby.

Did you know
babies prefer the sound of the human voice to all other sounds?

At birth the baby's ability to hear is developed, and as such, hearing a human voice acts as a bridge between baby and the unfamiliar, cold and strange world. Initially baby responds more to the tonality and inflection in your voice than to your words. She may not understand your words, but she certainly does understand the warmth, gentleness and kindness in your voice. It's your voice and your touch that form your baby's first social bonds and sense of self. It's through your touch and your voice that baby experiences acceptance and starts to develop a positive self-image!

So often moms and dads feel helpless, inadequate and ignorant about what to do with a newborn baby. For some, the first year or so until baby can talk seems to be a waste of time – but, of course, it's everything but. The first two years of a baby's life is, in fact, filled with more formative structural development than will probably take place in the rest of his life. It can best be illustrated by thinking about the Chinese bamboo. This plant is said to grow only one centimetre in the first year. After careful nurturing it grows another centimetre in the second year. With infinite patience and care it grows another centimetre in the third year. Three years with a maximum yield of three centimetres, but in the fourth year it shoots up by ten metres! How do you explain this sudden success?

In the first three years of the life of the bamboo, the main focus was on developing the intricate root system that would be needed to support, nourish and sustain the growth spurt in the fourth year. The same is true for human development. Animals are sturdy and reasonably independent soon after birth, but it takes the human baby many years to become independent due to the complexity of the mental growth spurt that occurs between the ages of four and eleven.

The window of opportunity for the optimal development of language and thought presents itself during the mental growth spurt between four and eleven. To enable baby to make full use of this opportunity, it is preceded by more or less four years of physical, social, emotional and language development necessary for supporting and sustaining mental development. It is this state of readiness and level of maturity which result in academic achievement.

Cognitive development

We have covered physical, social and emotional development. The outstanding component needed as a prerequisite for rational thought is language development.

There are two important steps in language development. The first step is to hear and understand language, and the second step is to produce language.

To be able to hear language, a baby's ears need to be stimulated as discussed on page 38 and 56. It's only once the ears can receive sound that language and speech can start developing.

As in the case of physical, social and emotional development, language gradually and steadily develops through interaction with people and the direct environment. Language develops through experiencing language, and therefore babies tend to echo their environment and as such, reflect what they are exposed to. Have you noticed how upset a baby gets when people are arguing? Babies are experts at hearing and reflecting emotional states!

Once baby can hear the nuances in sound and discriminate between different sounds, she is ready to learn the symbolic code called language.

From birth, baby starts producing sound by crying and making noises. It's amazing to notice how many variations of crying a baby can produce – some cries are for comfort, others for food or to indicate pain and others to exercise the speech organs.

By the age of four months, baby has extended her repertoire and her communication skills also include cooing noises. Most parents find cooing irresistible and respond by echoing the cooing which leads to elaborate exchanges that can last quite a while. The content of this primal conversation is completely unknown, but it forms the basis of communication, and as such, is crucial to baby's development. As baby experiments with sound through gurgling and cooing, she develops neurochemical branches to control the muscles of the

BabyGym – Brain and body gym for babies

larynx (speech box). Babbling is the first stage of speech development and differs from other noises made in that it is characterised by repetitive sounds of an immense variety. Baby's ability to match what she is hearing with the sound she is producing is the beginning of communication. She soon learns that certain sounds refer to or mean certain things, and that sounds are meant to communicate a request. As her words produce the desired outcome, so her vocabulary expands.

At more or less the sixth to the eighth month, the range of vocalisation grows rapidly and babies spend hours practising the sounds they can produce. Not all these sounds are human phonemes (functional speech-sounds) and not all of them are found in language to which is exposed.

Did you know

the sounds that English and Japanese babies produce are alike at this stage? According to research, even deaf babies babble, though less frequently.

These facts suggest that babies are born with the potential to learn any language if exposed to it.

When baby is ten or twelve months old, the range of sounds becomes more culture specific. Babbling now takes on the characteristics of the language baby is exposed to. Babbling now consists of reduplicated syllables like *mamama*, *dadada*, *nanana* or *papapa*. It is no accident that most cultures have chosen as their names for Mom and Dad some variant of *papa* or *mama*. These sounds coincide with sounds that baby can produce most easily at the end of the first year.

Cognitive development

It is important that language development should proceed steadily and that it does not matter whether the pace is fast or slow. Stages for speech development may be worrying if they are interpreted too rigidly. The speed of language development depends upon whether a baby is precocious (or ahead of her peers) and whether baby is left or right-brain dominant.

Did you know
left-brain dominant babies tend to talk sooner and walk later, while right-brain dominant babies tend to walk earlier and talk later?

BabyGym — Brain and body gym for babies

Sometime between month nine and month fifteen, baby starts using words to draw attention, demand an object or ask for attention. These words mostly describe baby's possessions, things that can move or things that baby can move. It may seem as if baby learns a word and then forgets it quickly, giving rise to a phenomenon called '*a word a week*', until all of a sudden all the words emerge round about baby's second birthday, resulting in a phenomenal word spurt.

Language is the source of thought. When babies master language, they gain the potential to:

- Name objects and, in so doing, create a sense of consistence, permanence and security;
- Organise perceptions and memory;
- Master more complex forms of reflection on objects, people and situations;
- Gain the capacity to share experiences with others;
- Deploy knowledge; and
- Learn to gain knowledge of occurrences and objects of which they have no direct experience through reading and writing.

How to stimulate language development

- From the moment you hold your baby in your arms, look baby in the eye and start talking to her as though she understands every word you say.
- Tell baby how much you love her.
- Smile, rock and coo to establish and maintain communication.
- Tell baby what your plans are for the day.
- Name objects and repeat the names often.
- Echo baby's cooing sounds and tonality.
- Make, and maintain, eye contact when talking to baby.
- Refrain from using baby language.
- Teach simple action rhymes that are often repeated.
- Tell or read short stories.
- Point out colours, shapes and numbers.
- Share interesting facts about animals and nature.

Cognitive development

- When you ask baby a question, wait for a response and then 'answer'. For example, when you ask baby if she wants more food, pause and then add, "Yes, it would be nice", or "No more, thank you".
- Express your feelings clearly and give reasons for feeling the way you do whenever you can.
- Record your baby's voice and sayings on video, audio cassette or in a journal. Their ability to generalise concepts and create words is impressive and to be treasured. Children love watching themselves or listening to themselves, not to mention how Grandpa and Grandma living far away would appreciate such information.

BabyGym — Brain and body gym for babies

A few words in closing

To stimulate babies' development, it is important to:

- Provide as many opportunities as possible for full sensory experiences – real experiences like going on outings, not book, television or computer experiences;
- Talk about these experiences, especially everyday occurrences like bathing, feeding and dressing;
- Repeat experiences to create a sense of familiarity;
- Constant use and repetition is the key to creating a safe and familiar environment in which baby can grow and glow.

BabyGym only focuses on the formative years from birth till baby's second birthday. It is the time when the necessary structural support systems like the body, the emotions, social skills and language are developed for optimal growth. This is the time when moms and dads need to remember the Chinese bamboo, and that every day counts even when there is no apparent evidence of growth. It is with this crucial time period in mind that the book gives you ideas on **how to** make every moment count.

These are also the years when you realise that your behaviour and actions speak much louder than your words. You are your baby's role model and bridge into the future. To guide your behaviour and actions spiritual healer and author Helene Rothschild wrote the following poem …

BabyGym – Brain and body gym for babies

Help me grow

Please ...
Be consistent with me. Then I can trust your words and actions.

Comfort me when I'm scared, hurt or sad. That will help me feel I'm okay even when I'm not feeling strong or happy.

Take responsibility for all your feelings and actions. That will teach me not to blame others and to take responsibility for my life.

Communicate what you feel hurt or frightened about when you're angry at me. That helps me feel I'm a good person, and learn how to constructively deal with my feelings.

Tell me clearly and specifically what you want. Then it is easier for me to hear you, and I will also know how to communicate my needs in a positive way.

Express to me that I'm okay even when my words or behavior may not be. That will help me learn from my mistakes, and have high self-esteem.

Understand and accept me. I may be different than you and I'm okay.

Balance your life between work and play. Then it is easier for me to believe that I can grow up, be responsible, and still have fun.

Remember what you wanted when you were my age. Then you'll better understand my needs and interests.

Treat me as an individual. That helps me believe that I can be my unique self.

Hug me and tell me that you care about me. That feels so good, and helps me feel lovable and express caring to others.

Thank you for hearing me. I love you!

A few words in closing

Guidelines for quick reference

It cannot but be repeated that every baby unfolds and develops at his own pace. Because your baby was not delivered with a customised how-to-raise-me manual, guidelines on what to expect at what age can be handy. But remember: These are **guidelines** only, as there is a wide range in normal development. Should your baby develop a month or so earlier or later than indicated, it is fine and no cause for concern. What is important is steady progress with the sequence of the progress as indicated in the following guidelines.

While there might well be some overlap with the preceding chapters, where parents were encouraged to enhance the natural flow of development, this chapter is intended to alert parents to possible delays or deviations.

> **Important note:** Premature babies develop according to the age they would be if they were born on the due date. To calculate your premature baby's developmental age:
>
> Baby is .... months old.
>
> Baby was born .... months premature.
>
> The difference between the two numbers is ....
>
> This number represents your baby's developmental age and generally applies until baby is two years old.

The developmental sequences of the most important functions are described separately to help you map your baby's progress in each of these crucial developmental stages. Should your baby not reach a specific developmental stage, you can use these guidelines to stimulate your baby's reflexes and growth to reach the desired outcome/milestone.

DEVELOPMENT OF CRAWLING

A baby should be able to crawl by week 44, but the sequence of steps to get baby to the crawling stage starts soon after birth, while in prone position.

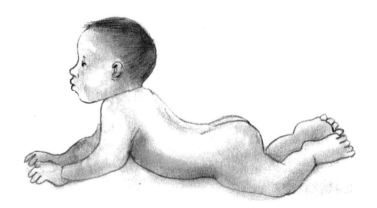

Birth to three months
1. Baby lies on his tummy in the prone position and turns his head to the side.
2. Still in prone position, baby lifts his head up for a moment.
3. The upright position of the head is the foundation of all essential movements as the head leads the way in all movement.

Three to six months

1. Baby supports himself on his forearms in the prone position.
2. Baby gradually starts supporting himself on his hands and no longer on the forearms.
3. The body weight now rests on the hands and tummy, and the head and chest are raised.
4. Baby moves around on his own axis, reaches out for objects and rolls over.
5. He starts creeping forward in a motion similar to that of a frog swimming.
6. Learning to crawl overlaps with learning to sit, and baby soon finds himself reaching too far for a toy and ends up on all fours.

Six to nine months

1. Finding himself on all fours, baby starts rocking forwards and backwards before collapsing on his tummy.
2. Baby rocks for a couple of days to try out his balancing reactions until he can control his body position, before a hand is ventured forward to set movement in motion.
3. Note that it is perfectly normal for babies to crawl a little backwards before they start moving forwards.

Nine to eleven months
1. Baby eventually succeeds in simultaneously bringing an arm and a leg forward without toppling over.
2. Gradually crawling becomes more secure, confident and rhythmic, and after a few weeks, baby conquers the entire house on all fours.

THE BENEFITS OF CRAWLING

Crawling marks the end of primitive movement and fulfils an extremely important developmental function. Crawling on all fours exercises the gross-motor muscles, co-ordinates the muscles and the balancing reactions, and integrates the left and right brain as pre-requisites for walking. Crawling also exercises and stabilises the shoulder girdle as the basis for later fine-motor control, re-

Guidelines for quick reference

quired for actions like putting blocks in a shape holder or holding a crayon. Crawling, moreover, is the first step in goal setting and planning action-steps to achieve the goal. In addition, crawling assists in spatial orientation, which helps in knowing left from right and, when writing, to avoid the reversal of letters like *b*, *d* and *p*.

DEVELOPMENT OF SITTING

Baby should be able to sit and play confidently by week 30. Sitting goes together with hand movements like eating and playing, and requires a lot of strength and co-ordination. To be able to sit, baby needs to be able to keep his head up and turn it in all directions; the hips need to be flexible and the trunk must be able to rotate (hip and shoulders working separately).

BabyGym – Brain and body gym for babies

Birth to three months

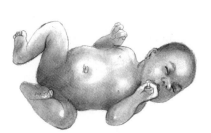

1. When a newborn baby lies on his back (supine position), the head lies to the side.
2. Baby starts turning his head to mid-position to look forward.
3. After a few weeks, baby is able to hold his head and face forward for a prolonged period.
4. Baby now also starts turning his face towards a person or a sound.
5. Baby's head flops back when you try to pull him into a sitting position by his arms.
6. By the end of the third month, baby can hold his head up for more than thirty seconds, even though it may still flop unexpectedly.
7. Flexibility in the hips develops simultaneously with head stability, and can best be seen when a baby kicks energetically with both legs from birth onwards.

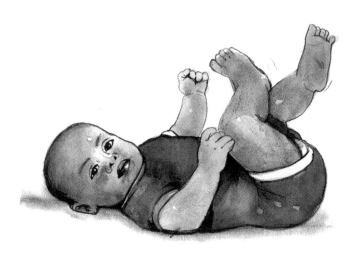

Guidelines for quick reference

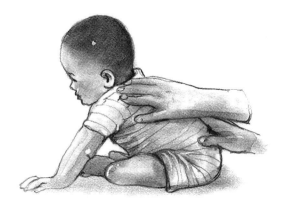

Three to six months

1. When baby is drawn up into the sitting position, the spine lengthens and the head is brought forward.

2. The head is held upright more frequently as the muscles strengthen and stability improves.

3. The vestibular apparatus (balance system in ear) helps the brain to register the position of the head.

4. When you gently hold your baby in a sitting position and push him slightly to the left or the right, the head will follow the body and, after a while, start moving back to centre to right himself into the upright position.

5. Normally the head can be held perfectly stable by the sixth month.

6. Usually at this stage, hip flexibility is on par when a wide range of leg movements also include the ability to hold the legs up in a vertical position for a few seconds at a time.

7. Baby starts grasping his feet and knees, and thus explores new parts of the body.

8. Baby completes the prerequisites for sitting by rolling over from his back onto his tummy.

BabyGym – Brain and body gym for babies

Six to nine months

1. Enough rug-time allows baby to roll over and, with time and practice, start supporting himself on his forearms.
2. After a while, he starts supporting his weight with an extended arm on his hand while spreading his legs to establish a stable base.
3. His newly developed tummy and back muscles come to his aid in attempting to raise his body up into an upright position.
4. Initially he may lean forward and support his body on both hands, but soon his balance and co-ordination allow him to sit upright.

Nine to ten months

1. Baby masters the skill of sitting unsupported with extended legs and arms moving about freely.
2. He can now turn his body in all directions to explore his environment.

THE BENEFITS OF SITTING

Sitting is an important milestone to reach as it is from the stability of the sitting position that a baby starts developing new visual positions and hand co-ordination. Being able to sit enables baby to develop the all-important eye-hand co-ordination necessary for playing, drawing and for writing and reading at a later age.

Guidelines for quick reference

DEVELOPMENT OF WALKING

The art of walking is mastered some-where between baby's first birthday and fourteen months of age, but starts developing soon after birth. It takes a baby more or less ten months to attain an upright position, and only thereafter can he start the last leg of the journey to becoming part of the species *Homo sapiens* (modern man who walks up-right).

Birth to three months

1. Newborn babies can walk reflexively for the first two months when you hold them gently, but firmly, under the armpits in an upright position. When the feet touch a surface they will au-tomatically make stepping movements alternately with each leg.
2. This reflex disappears around the second month when the leg muscles have been exercised sufficiently to not pull up into a foetal position.
3. Now your baby's legs remain bent and refuse to stand when the feet touch a surface. This is normal and can last for a few weeks.

BabyGym – Brain and body gym for babies

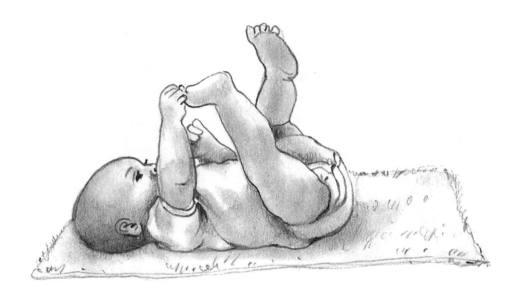

Three to six months

1. Baby's unfailing enthusiasm in practising his kicking to strengthen the legs, his hip flexibility, and his lengthened spine due to head control, result in pre-walking readiness.

2. When you hold him, he can now stand and bear his body weight for a second or two.

3. His head is upright, but his posture is still slightly bent and his toes may 'claw' to maintain his balance.

4. After a few weeks of building strength and confidence, baby discovers the joy of bouncing.

Six to nine months

1. Bouncing starts off as a sagging in the knees followed by an upwards thrust, actions which soon change into full-blown bouncing.
2. Do not lift baby from a squatting position, but allow him to push himself up to lengthen his hips, knees and ankles.
3. Bouncing on your lap is good, as your legs and baby's muscles will know when it is enough. Suspended jumping apparatus are not recommended.
4. Near the end of his ninth month, baby should be able to stand for thirty seconds if held by the hands, **not** the body or arms – feet should be flat, soles touching the surface.

BabyGym – Brain and body gym for babies

Nine to ten months

1. Baby soon ventures to stand on his own, pulling himself up while holding on to something.
2. His time spent in practising to stand up, flopping back down on his bottom only to get up once again, also serves as the foundation for resilience – a life skill needed right throughout life.
3. Baby starts shifting his body weight onto one leg, while placing the other leg towards the side. Body weight is then shifted and the leg is dragged to start movement/cruising.
4. Cruising around the furniture becomes his favourite game and creates the necessary opportunity to co-ordinate the legs and enjoy being upright.

Guidelines for quick reference

Ten to twelve months

1. Baby loves holding on to Mom or Dad's hands and attempts a step or two forward. The hips are normally pushed forward and the legs are dragged, but nevertheless, baby is starting to 'walk'.

2. Every now and then, baby starts experimenting with standing unaided. As is the case when he is learning to crawl, he starts rocking gently forwards and backwards, landing on his behind every so often.

3. All of a sudden, one day the rocking becomes the first step.

4. Within days you cannot believe that a short week ago he couldn't walk at all!

5. Contrary to general belief, only 60% of babies can walk by their first birthday. Some start walking at nine months and others at sixteen months. Walking is one of the most variable milestones and should not be used as a measure of intelligence or developmental success. Normally a left-brain dominant baby talks earlier than the norm, and a right-brain dominant baby walks earlier than the norm.

BabyGym – Brain and body gym for babies

THE BENEFITS OF WALKING

Walking marks the transition period where a baby moves from discovering himself and his body, to discovering the environment, objects and people. He now reaches out to expand his territory and finds his world a source of constant stimulation and fun. New objects mean new words and his vocabulary expands rapidly. This is a time of discovery and nothing is perceived as out of bounds. Ensure your home is child-safe!

DEVELOPMENT OF LANGUAGE

Language builds bridges between people, creating a sense of belonging and acceptance. It also enables the transferral of knowledge and cultural heritage, and thus language is a cornerstone of social development.

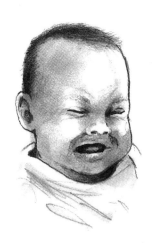

From birth, a baby expresses himself through a vast array of sounds and cries. These sounds and cries may not be perceived as language, but they are important steps towards language acquisition.

Birth to two months
1. Babies tend to sleep for long periods of time during the first two months, and they communicate mainly through loud crying.
2. They may also produce vowels and guttural sounds.
3. Sucking presents them with excellent opportunities to develop their facial muscles, lips and tongue – all used in the formation of sounds and words at a later stage.

Guidelines for quick reference

Two to four months

1. Babies experiment more frequently with sounds, and strings of *r-r-r* sounds, as if they are gargling, are often produced.
2. The first syllables, like *ma*, *da*, *pa* and *ta* become clear.
3. Baby is pacified when talked to in a soothing voice, and starts smiling.
4. At times he may squeal with joy, expressing satisfaction, or shout out loud, expressing discomfort.
5. A constant talking companion is crucial.

BabyGym – Brain and body gym for babies

Four to six months

1. Baby responds to his name.
2. He looks at you when you talk to him.
3. He tries to talk through babbling – stringing together familiar vowels and consonants.
4. He starts imitating your speech by varying his pitch and volume while babbling.
5. He responds appropriately to angry and friendly tones.
6. He becomes selective about whom he talks to and prefers talking to his family and primary caregivers.
7. He also loves babbling when he is alone and content.

Six to twelve months

1. Baby tends to understand a few words, such as *ta-ta*, when they are accompanied with gestures.
2. He starts repeating sounds that have already been expressed in previous months. These sounds resemble words that can be understood, such as *ma-ma*.
3. He also imitates you when you cough and sing.
4. Towards the end of the first year, first real words appear when baby forms a connection between an object or person and a set of sounds, for instance when Daddy comes home and he excitedly calls out, "Papa!".
5. *Woof-woof* may mean dog, but may also represent any four-legged animal.
6. Baby learns nouns first and verbs soon afterwards, hence the importance of constantly naming objects in the environment.

Twelve to eighteen months

1. Baby responds to simple requests such as: "Show me your nose".
2. He starts nodding his head to say, "Yes" and shaking his head to say, "No".
3. He loves rhythm, and dancing and singing become favourite pastimes.
4. He points at objects while making sounds to indicate his needs.
5. He says about ten words clearly.

Guidelines for quick reference

Eighteen to twenty-four months

1. He can name a couple of objects commonly found in his environment.
2. Baby strings two words together (usually noun-verb combinations) to create sentences.
3. He can ask for a favourite toy or food.
4. He understands many more words than he can use.
5. He can follow simple instructions, such as, "Eat your food" or, "Fetch me a nappy".
6. He is able to use at least two prepositions, for instance *in*, *under* or *on*.
7. *My* and *mine* are beginning to emerge.
8. At least 66% of what he says should be intelligible.
9. He could have a vocabulary of approximately 150 to 300 words.

BabyGym – Brain and body gym for babies

THE BENEFITS OF LANGUAGE DEVELOPMENT

Adequate language development in the early years is imperative for the development of thinking skills that are necessary for academic success. The baby first learns that words are names for concrete objects, later on he learns that words represent meaningful experiences, thereafter concept formation commences, for example, *suppertime* has a particular meaning. The thinking skills such as defining, analysis, comparison, classification, categorisation, organisation, memorising, evaluation, problem-solving, etc. are dependent on the development of concepts. Adequate language development is therefore the cornerstone of concept formation and mathematical ability.

Bibliography

Ayres, Jean. *Sensory Integration and the Child*. Los Angeles: Western Pscycho-logical Services, 1979.

Baba en Kleuter. "Mylpale van spraak". Article in February 2003 issue.

De Jager, Melodie. *Brain Gym for All*. Cape Town: Human & Rousseau, 2001.

De Jager, Melodie. *Mind Dynamics*. Cape Town: Human & Rousseau, 2002.

De Klerk, Rina and Le Roux, Ronél. *Emotional Intelligence for Children and Teens*. Cape Town: Human & Rousseau, 2003.

Dennison, Gail E. and Dennison, Paul E. *Brain Gym*. Ventura, CA: Edu-Kines-thetics, Inc., 1989.

Einon, D. *Learning Early*. London: Marshal Publishing, 1998.

Erickson, Erik H. *Toys and Reasons.* London: Marion Boyars Publishers Ltd., 1978.

Ginsburg, Herbet and Opper, Sylvia. *Piaget's Theory of Intellectual Develop-ment*. New Jersey: Prentice-Hall Inc., 1969.

Goleman, Daniel. *Emotional Intelligence*. London: Bloomsbury, 1996.

Hannaford, Carla. *Smart Moves*. Arlington, Virginia: Great Ocean Publishers, 1995.

Hellbrügge, Theodor. *The first 365 days in the life of a child*. Pretoria: The Baby Therapy Centre, 2002.

Johnson, Mark. *The Body in the Mind: The Bodily Basis of Meaning, Imagina-tion and Reason*. Chicago: University of Chicago Press, 1987.

Krantz, M. *Child Development*. Belmont, CA: Wadsworth, 1994.

Le Roux, Ronél and De Klerk, Rina. *Emotional Intelligence Workbook*. Cape Town: Human & Rousseau, 2001

MacLean, Paul D. *The Triune Brain in Evolution: Role in Paleo-Cerebral Functions*. New York: Plenum Press, 1990.

Sheridan, M.D. *From Birth to Five Years*. London: Routledge, 1991.

Walker, Peter. *Baby Massage*. Canada: CDG Books, 2000.

Yeats, Liz. *Communicating with Your Child*. Cape Town, Struik Publishers, 1991.

Index

BabyGym – Brain and body gym for babies

BabyGym — Brain and body gym for babies

Kinesthetics 24
Knowledge, deploying 94

Index

V

W

BabyGym – Brain and body gym for babies

Notes

....

....

....

....

....

....

....

....

....

....

....

BabyGym — Brain and body gym for babies